D is for Democracy

A Citizen's Alphabet

Written by Elissa Grodin and Illustrated by Victor Juhasz

(With Sleeping Bear Press), I wish to thank Professor Michael Schudson
(Department of Communication, University of California, San Diego)
and Thomas Collier (retired lecturer in history, University of Michigan)
for reading the manuscript with great care and offering comments of
terrific erudition and insight.

The book owes everything to Barbara McNally, who conceived of it,
and then, encouraged and shaped it into existence.

—*Elissa Grodin*

Sleeping Bear Press™

310 North Main Street, Suite 300
Chelsea, MI 48118
www.sleepingbearpress.com

THOMSON
—★—™
GALE

© 2007 Thomson Gale, a part of the Thomson Corporation.

Thomson, Star Logo and Sleeping Bear Press are trademarks
and Gale is a registered trademark used herein under license.

Printed and bound in Canada.

10 9 8 7 6 5 4 3 2 (pbk)
10 9 8 7 6 5 4 3 (case)

Library of Congress Cataloging-in-Publication Data

Grodin, Elissa, 1954-
D is for democracy : a citizen's alphabet / written by Elissa Grodin ;
illustrated by Victor Juhasz.
p. cm.

pbk ISBN 13: 978-1-58536-328-5   **case** ISBN 13: 978-1-58536-234-9
ISBN 10: 1-58536-328-6   ISBN 10: 1-58536-234-4

1. United States—Politics and government—Juvenile literature. 2. English
language—Alphabet—Juvenile literature. I. Juhasz, Victor, ill. II. Title.
JK40.G76 2004
320.973—dc22   2004005952

To Chuck and Nicky

ELISSA

★

For Woody Guthrie, Johnny Cash, and Howard Brodie—
three Americans who represent the Spirit of this Democracy.

VICTOR

A is for Amendment,
    a fancy word for change.
The Constitution's authors
    planned for us, long-range.

In the early 1900s Edna Purtell was an outspoken teenager known in her community for being someone not afraid to stand up for what she thought was right. Edna didn't think it was fair that women couldn't vote, and she was willing to do something about it, from printing up pamphlets to marching in demonstrations.

In its early days, this social movement to get the vote for women was linked to another civil right: abolition. Many courageous women, among them Elizabeth Cady Stanton, Sojourner Truth, Harriet Tubman, and Susan B. Anthony, worked hard to change the laws. In 1865 the Thirteenth Amendment made slavery illegal, and in 1920 the Nineteenth Amendment finally gave women the right to vote.

The framers of our Constitution understood that as society changed, the Constitution would need to be flexible enough to change along with it. Amendments are changes in the law. The word "amend" means to make a change or correct an error. The framers made it possible, but not easy, to change the fundamental law of the land. The Nineteenth Amendment was introduced to Congress 118 times and it took 30 years to pass into law. More than 10,000 amendments have been proposed since 1789, but only 27 have made it into law.

Aa

The United States Constitution is a document much admired around the world. It was written after the War of Independence with England, and it was approved in 1789. It reflects the principles on which our system of government is based. Do you know what a blueprint for a house is? The Constitution and Bill of Rights are a blueprint for a democratic society. The group of men who worked on the Constitution is called the Founding Fathers. They met over a period of months at the Constitutional Convention in Philadelphia in 1787. Their goal was to create a government for a society whose citizens would be able to live together harmoniously but still have personal freedom.

Shortly after the Constitution was signed, the Bill of Rights was added. Thomas Jefferson and others felt that the Constitution did not completely guarantee individual liberties and freedom for its citizens. The first 10 amendments to the Constitution make up the Bill of Rights. The first amendment, perhaps the best known, guarantees freedom of speech, freedom of religion, freedom of the press, and freedom of assembly.

B b

B is for the Bill of Rights—
The freedom to express
ideas and opinions
and how we want to dress.

C c

C is for the Congress
where committees are a must.
Ideas for new laws
are thoroughly discussed.

The Founding Fathers had a good understanding of human nature. They designed a system of government that has three branches. Each one keeps track of the other, so no one person or group can get too much power. This is called "checks and balances."

The three branches are the legislative, executive, and judicial. The legislative branch makes our laws, the executive branch is responsible for carrying out the laws, and the judicial branch makes sure that all the laws are in keeping with the Constitution.

Congress is part of the legislative branch. Its main function is to make federal (national) laws. The Congress is located in the United States Capitol in Washington, D.C. It has been holding its sessions there since 1800. Congress is made up of two "houses," the House of Representatives and the Senate, each with lots of committees, working on many areas of law. Before a new law is passed, it is first presented as a bill in either house. Each year Congress works on thousands of bills, but only a very small percentage of them become laws.

Officially a republic, our system of government is called a democracy. It is based on the United States Constitution, a document written hundreds of years ago by the Founding Fathers. They based the Constitution on the philosophy that "all men are created equal."

What does that mean? Everything written can be interpreted in different ways. If every citizen should have equal rights under the law, what about slaves? Slaves were not considered citizens initially in American society.

Part of the genius of the Constitution is that it was written in a way that allowed for changes to be made to it, through a dialogue with its citizenry. Amendment Thirteen abolished slavery in 1865, making it un-Constitutional.

It is important to understand the reasons the early colonists came to America in the first place. They were fleeing from a government that did not allow its citizens enough individual rights, such as practicing whatever religion they chose, or pursuing economic freedom. Some people wanted a life where they could be more than servants to a king. Our economic system is called capitalism, which means that private citizens can own businesses and industries.

D is for Democracy,
   where citizens can choose
whom they wish to vote for
   and freely share their views.

The early activists were willing to work hard and even fight for what they believed in. They paved the way for the freedoms and liberties we enjoy today, for example your right at this very moment to disagree with something in our government, and not get arrested for it!

Democracy in America is considered today one of the best books ever written on the subject. It is full of perceptive observations and comments about our democracy. Believe it or not, this book was written long ago, in 1835, by a Frenchman.

Alexis de Tocqueville (1805-1859) was a young aristocrat who came to America to learn everything he could about our democratic system. Monsieur de Tocqueville grew up in the aftermath of the French Revolution, and he wanted to help teach people back home in Europe about our American system of democracy. His book was the result of nine months of traveling all over our nation.

E is for Elections—
We're guaranteed this right.
It often gets exciting
counting votes all night.

Elections are held to choose officials at local, state, and national levels. Local elections in towns, cities, and counties select citizens for positions such as mayor, city council, sheriff, and school board members. At the state level, elections are held to select a governor, state legislators, and judges, although in some states judges are appointed for life. Elections at the national level select our president, vice president, and members of Congress.

Since there are always a number of candidates from each political party who want to run for president, primary elections are held to pick delegates to represent the candidates of their choice. Then delegates, who represent every voting district, go to the national convention to select their party's candidate.

Every four years, national elections are held on the first Tuesday after the first Monday in November. State and local elections are held every year on many different days.

American voting methods have changed over the years. In the early days, vote counts were often taken with people announcing their candidate of choice out loud. Later, voting consisted of endorsing one or another party by putting that party's "ticket" in a ballot box. It was in the 1890s that voters began choosing candidates from printed ballots.

In 1787 55 delegates from 12 states met in Philadelphia for a national convention that lasted several months. This was the Constitutional Convention. Many of the delegates were lawyers as well as plantation owners, soldiers, merchants, doctors, and scientists. Engaged in long debates and heated disagreements, their purpose was to figure out how to form a government that would best protect the freedoms of every citizen. By the end of the convention they had drafted the Constitution. The following men played key roles in the development of our democratic government.

George Washington (1732-1799) was unanimously elected to preside over the Constitutional Convention. Said to be good at resolving disagreements because of his wise and calm manner, Washington went on to serve two terms as president.

A deep and dazzling thinker, Thomas Jefferson (1743-1826) spoke brilliantly on the subject of our independence from England. Aside from minor alterations made by Ben Franklin and John Adams, Jefferson was the author of the Declaration of Independence. He was our third president.

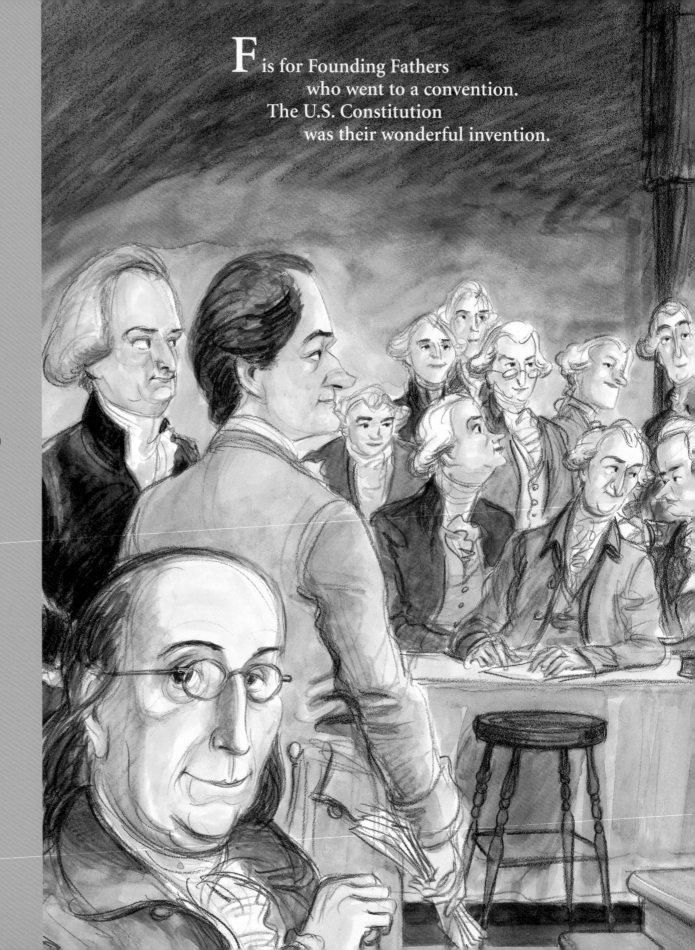

F is for Founding Fathers
who went to a convention.
The U.S. Constitution
was their wonderful invention.

Benjamin Franklin (1706-1790) had left school at the age of 10, and gone on to study languages, science, and philosophy, and become an inventor. He signed the Declaration of Independence, helped work on the Constitution, and served overseas as an American diplomat.

John Adams (1735-1826) was a brilliant revolutionary who spoke beautifully and forcefully in support of the Declaration of Independence, which he helped outline. Adams was our second president.

A visionary statesman who wrote persuasive articles on the subject of colonial independence, Alexander Hamilton (1755-1804) understood the importance of a strong national government. He played a huge role in forming our domestic and foreign policy.

James Madison (1751-1836) urged a strong central government and, with a magnificent understanding of government and political philosophy, he had the ability to persuade others. Madison earned the title "Master Builder of the Constitution." He was our fourth president.

Gg

G is for the Government,
the way our country's run:
With liberties and rights
enjoyed by everyone.

The word 'democracy' comes from the ancient Greek, *demos* (people) and *kratos* (power). This is where democracy first flourished, especially in the city of Athens, where citizens participated directly in law-making. Because the majority of people at that time were slaves or noncitizens, the number of citizens enjoying the democratic system was small. It was a *limited democracy*.

The philosophical heart of our democratic system of government rests on a very important idea. It's a simple idea: We the people possess political power. Ultimate authority doesn't come from up above, from a king or a religious figure. The supreme political power rests in the hands of the citizenry, of you and me.

Nondemocratic societies are not concerned with the idea that citizens should be allowed to participate in government. In a totalitarian system, for example, one person, a dictator, has total authority over the population. There are no checks and balances in this type of government. In a monarchy, a sovereign (king or queen) rules the country. Great Britain is a *constitutional monarchy*, where the king or queen's power is limited, and elected officials run the government.

"The House" is one of two chambers that make up Congress. The other is the Senate. The number of representatives from each state to the House is based on population. The greater the population in a state, the more representatives to the House. The elected term is two years, but a representative may be reelected an unlimited amount of times. Anyone can try to get elected as representative: a teacher, a farmer, an electrician, anybody, as long as they are 25 years of age or older. There are 435 representatives in the House.

The two chambers of Congress, the House and the Senate, share equal power but have different functions. Whichever political party has more elected members in the House is called the majority party. That party elects the Speaker of the House, who is in charge of all its activities. Work on new bills and laws is done by committee, with Democrats and Republicans working together.

H is for House of Representatives
where all sorts of committees
work on laws protecting folks
in suburbs, towns, and cities.

FINE HOWARD COSTELLO ABBOTT JONES

I is for Immigration.
Tired of all the strife,
people leave their homes
to find a better life.

What does it take to be a U.S. citizen? If you were not born here, or your parents weren't citizens, it is still possible to become an American citizen.

To come to the United States in hopes of becoming naturalized, you must first apply for a visa from the American Embassy in your country. When you arrive here you must show that you have a place to live and a job. After living here for five years, providing you haven't been in any legal trouble, you can apply to become a citizen. You must be able to read and speak English. You must pass a test proving that you understand the duties and rights of an American citizen. Finally, you must take an oath, given by a federal judge, promising to fulfill the duties of an American citizen. It is called the Oath of Allegiance.

The Fourteenth Amendment to the Constitution says all persons born or naturalized in the United States enjoy the rights of citizens.

Ii

J is for Judicial branch—
For justice, judge, and jury.
Those who do not break the law
never have to worry.

You might think the law is clear-cut, that a thing is either wrong or right, but the law is more complicated than that. Argument and debate over how to interpret the law is very common.

The Supreme Court is part of the judicial branch of our federal government, along with the lower federal courts. As the highest court in the land, its task is to study laws to make sure they are in keeping with the ideals of the Constitution. There are nine Supreme Court justices: eight associate justices, and one chief justice who decides which cases the Supreme Court will hear. The justices are nominated by the president, approved by the Senate, and appointed for life.

In 1954, when much of our society was racially segregated, five African-American families filed lawsuits against their local school districts. They wanted their children to be allowed to attend the all-white schools, where they would receive better educations. The case, Brown v. Board of Education, went all the way to the Supreme Court, where it was ruled that segregation is unconstitutional under the Fourteenth Amendment. This amendment forbids laws that unfairly deny citizens their rights. This important decision paved the way for a flurry of new civil rights laws in the following years.

Kk

K is for Dr. King,
who worked for what was right.
He knew that using peaceful ways
was better than a fight.

After the Supreme Court ruled that segregated schools were unconstitutional, things did not exactly go smoothly. Even though the Constitution provides equal rights under the law for all citizens, sometimes human nature makes it difficult to enforce. The civil rights movement was a reaction to exactly that.

Martin Luther King Jr. was a black minister who became a civil rights activist, devoted to protecting peoples' constitutional freedoms. He believed in nonviolent methods of protest, such as economic boycotts (refusal to buy a certain product or service) and peaceful demonstrations. In 1955 in Montgomery, Alabama, he organized a boycott against the segregated bus lines. Nearly all the black people refused to ride the buses and walked to work instead. It was a terrible hardship but they were determined to change an unfair situation. It worked. After 381 days of boycott, the bus company agreed to run on a desegregated basis. In 1963 Dr. King organized a huge demonstration in Washington, D.C. that successfully pressured Congress into passing new civil rights legislation.

Dr. King traveled the country, organizing marches and protests and teaching peaceful resistance wherever people were being denied their civil rights. In 1964 he received the Nobel Peace Prize for his nonviolent leadership. Sadly, Dr. King was assassinated in 1968.

The role of First Lady is a very interesting one: Even though we don't elect our First Lady, it is considered by many to be one of the most powerful positions any woman can hold. This full-time, unpaid job has evolved and changed a lot over the years. After all, there is no real job description.

Martha Washington was 58 years old when she became the First Lady in 1789. A very private person who at first felt shy in her public position, Mrs. Washington made the best of her new role. Her natural grace and style helped set the standard for First Ladies to follow. The early First Ladies focused mainly on their social duties as official hostess. Although this remains an important aspect, eventually First Ladies began to pursue their own interests. When she was in the White House (1889-1893), Caroline Harrison agreed to raise money for Johns Hopkins University Medical School if it would admit women. Eleanor Roosevelt (1933-1945) worked tirelessly to promote civil rights for minorities, and to draw attention to unemployment and poor housing.

What title do you think we should use for the husband of the first female president?

L1

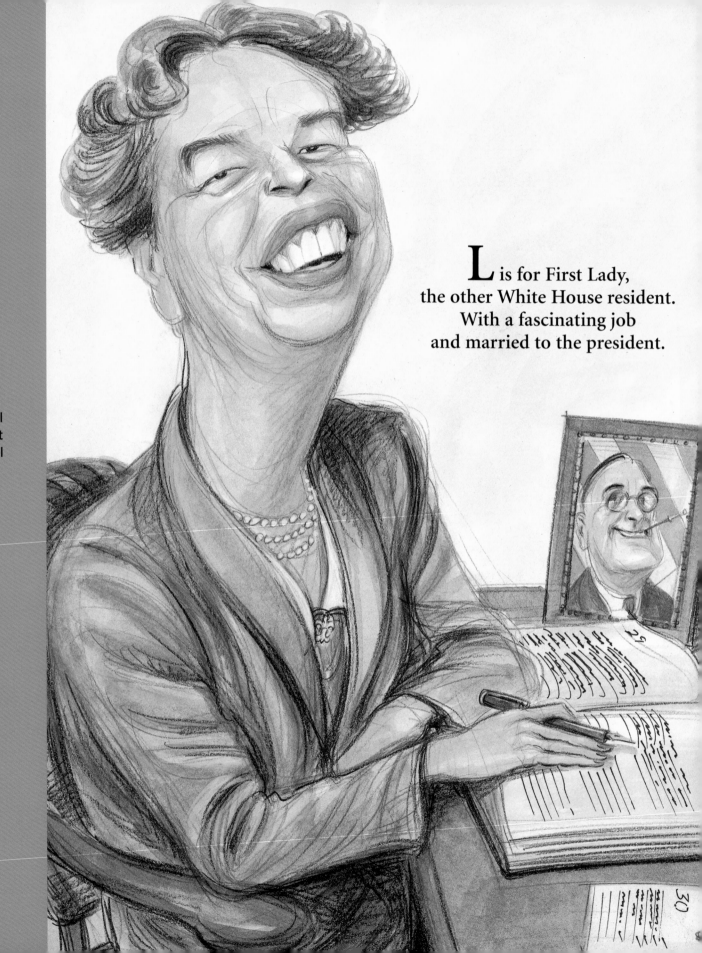

L is for First Lady,
the other White House resident.
With a fascinating job
and married to the president.

Mm

Before there was the Mint a curious variety of things were used as currency by the early colonists, including livestock, tobacco, and foreign currency.

Congress created the United States Mint in 1792, and President George Washington appointed David Rittenhouse its first director. To "mint" a coin means to stamp it with a design. Also established that year were the Mint Police. Today the Mint Police are one of the oldest federal law enforcement agencies in the country, responsible for protecting over $100 billion.

The Mint is part of the United States Treasury Department, which also oversees the Bureau of Engraving and Printing (they manufacture paper money), the Internal Revenue Service (tax collection), and surprisingly, the Secret Service. The reason for this is that during the disruption and chaos of the Civil War, some banks began printing their own money. The Treasury Department needed an investigative agency to track down all the thousands of counterfeit claims.

M is for the Mint,
and printed money, too,
that ends up in the pockets
of folks like me and you.

N is for our Nation's capital—
Where everyone agrees
it's delightful to behold
the famous cherry trees.

When George Washington was elected president in 1789, he and Martha first lived in New York City. That summer they moved to the temporary capital in Philadelphia. In 1790 the president was asked to pick a location for our young country's permanent capital city. He chose a beautiful spot along the Potomac River, near his family home in Virginia.

Although he never lived there, Washington, D.C. is named after our first president. The District of Columbia is named in honor of Christopher Columbus. Washington, D.C. is located in a 68-square-mile parcel between Maryland and Virginia. When President John Adams became the first resident in the White House on November 2, 1800, Washington was a rural setting where cows grazed along roads and cornfields stood among the houses.

Today Washington is a fascinating place to visit. Due to a law that states that no building may be higher than the Washington Monument (555 feet), Washington has no skyscrapers, giving it a feeling of wide-open beauty. Our capital is scattered with remarkable museums and national monuments of beauty and grace. The most famous natural attraction is the cherry blossoms, on display in the springtime. The cherry trees were a gift from the mayor of Tokyo in 1912.

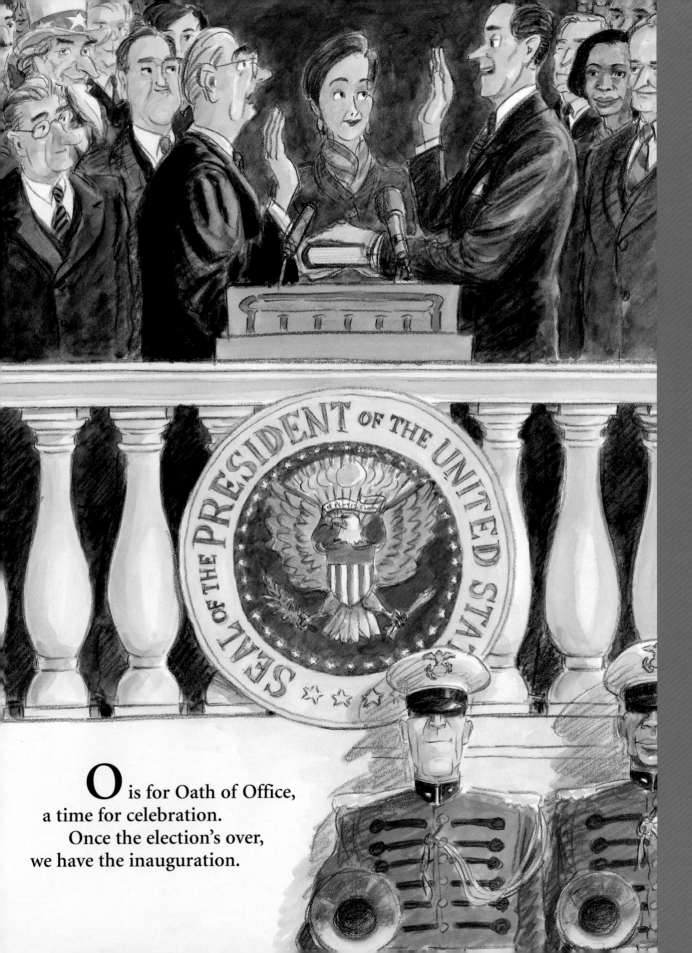

O is for Oath of Office,
a time for celebration.
Once the election's over,
we have the inauguration.

At 12:00 noon on January 20 in the year following a presidential election, the new president is sworn into office at the Inauguration ceremony. He takes the Oath of Office, which is administered by the Chief Justice of the Supreme Court at the United States Capitol building. After he is sworn in, the new president makes an inaugural speech. In President John F. Kennedy's 1961 inaugural speech he uttered the now-famous words, "Ask not what your country can do for you; ask what you can do for your country."

All elected and appointed officials, from mayors to presidents, are required to take an oath of office. Your town's Board of Education members, postmaster, and police chief all promised to uphold the law when they took their sworn oaths.

Presidential Oath of Office:

I do solemnly swear (or affirm) that I will faithfully execute the office of President of the United States, and will to the best of my ability, preserve, protect, and defend the Constitution of the United States.

Pp

What is a political party? It sounds sort of fun, doesn't it, but the word 'party' is misleading. A political party is simply a group of people who generally agree about what kinds of decisions, laws, and policies the government should make. In other words, the members of a political party are in basic agreement about the best way to run the country. Their set of ideas is called a "platform."

Interestingly, President George Washington was against the idea of different parties, but even in his day, two separate parties did form: the Federalists and the Democratic-Republicans. These days the two major parties are the Democrats and Republicans. Each has a mascot or symbol. The Republicans' is an elephant and the Democrats,' a donkey. Both symbols were created in the 1870s by political cartoonist Thomas Nast.

A political party is not like a club that you join. It is more like a philosophy that you agree with. Republicans and Democrats can agree on some things, and disagree on others. They do have one basic disagreement. Democrats think the government should be of assistance to citizens who need its help, through social programs like welfare. Republicans, who also want to help people, think assistance should not come primarily from the government, but from private companies and individuals who are willing to help.

P is for Political Party,
with ideas that represent
    how the politicians
should run our government.

Besides the two main parties there are several others. The Green Party is committed to environmentalism, nonviolence, social justice, and grassroots organizing. They think big corporations have too much say in government, and that common people should have more power in policy-making for our country. The smaller Libertarian Party wants government to have practically no say at all in the private lives of citizens. People calling themselves Independents have no party affiliations.

Anyone can start his or her own party. What would be the philosophy and focus of yours?

The most effective citizens are those who are informed. This means reading newspapers, participating in discussions, and asking questions. After all, ours is "The peoples' government, made for the people, made by the people, and answerable to the people." (Daniel Webster 1782-1852)

The First Amendment to the Constitution guarantees the civil liberties we require to have a free and open dialogue with one another and with the elected officials in our government. Freedom of Speech is one such liberty. It gives us the authority to express our opinions even when they are in disagreement with the government. Freedom of Assembly entitles people to get together and share these opinions, as long as they do it peacefully, without causing harm to anyone. In some countries, meetings and organizations are controlled by the government, and people do not enjoy this freedom. We even have a law that helps journalists get information by allowing them access to government records. It is called the Freedom of Information Act.

Q is for the Questions
all of us should ask.
Taking part in a democracy
is every citizen's task.

Often the reason that early colonists came to America was to escape the tyranny of the Church of England. This official, established church was the law of the land, and English citizens were expected to obey its rules, as well as pay taxes to support it, whether they were believers or not.

When it came time to draft our Bill of Rights, the First Amendment took care to guarantee American citizens religious freedom. Everyone has the Constitutional right to practice whatever religion they choose or none at all. Along with this liberty goes the responsibility to protect the rights of others. It's important to stand up for anyone who is being treated unfairly because of religious practices or beliefs.

The three R's of religious freedom are: rights (every citizen's right to choose their religion), respect (respect others' religious choices), and responsibility (the obligation to protect the religious freedoms of others).

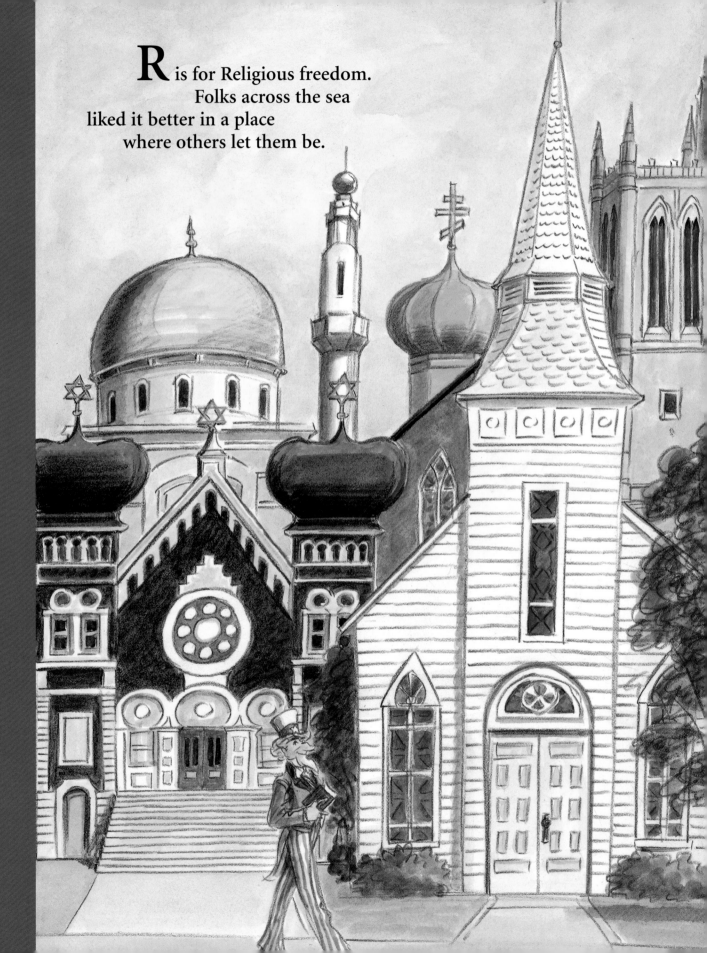

R is for Religious freedom.
Folks across the sea
liked it better in a place
where others let them be.

Part of the legislative (lawmaking) branch of government, the Senate is the other chamber of Congress, along with the House of Representatives. There are 100 senators, two from each state, serving six-year terms. A senator can be reelected an unlimited number of times. Besides meeting and talking with his or her own constituency (voters from the state) as much as possible, a senator's main job is to make laws that improve life for citizens.

A new law begins life as a bill, which may come from an idea suggested by one of the senator's constituents. The senator takes the bill to a few other senators who will cosponsor it. The senator next introduces the bill at a Senate session. If there is interest, the bill gets assigned to a subcommittee for review. The senator may ask experts to come and testify on behalf of the bill and may also encourage his constituents to write letters in support. If the subcommittee votes in favor of the bill, it then passes on to the rest of the Senate committee, where it is either approved or not. If approved, it will go before the entire Senate for a vote. If approved by both houses, it finally goes to the president, who has the power to approve or veto the bill.

S s

S is for the Senate
that helps communicate
the needs of all the people
from every single state.

Tt

T is for the Taxes:
No longer fees for kings,
   now our money helps to pay
for a thousand different things.

Income tax means that you pay a percentage of the money you earn each year (income) to the government. The government is like a business in the sense that it needs money to operate and pay for things: Some examples of programs and services handled by the government include education, defense, and social services such as Social Security. Taxes are collected to pay the government's operating costs.

There are many other kinds of taxes besides income tax. For example, you pay inheritance tax if someone gives you a large gift of money. If you own a house, you pay property taxes. Some states have sales tax when you buy things like bikes, clothes, cars, and furniture.

The Internal Revenue Service (IRS) is the official agency responsible for making sure everyone pays his fair share of taxes. No one really likes paying taxes, but refusing to do so can land you in jail. The beginnings of the IRS go back to the Civil War. In 1862 President Lincoln and Congress enacted an income tax to pay war expenses. The tax was repealed (taken away) 10 years later. In 1913 the Sixteenth Amendment was passed, authorizing income tax permanently.

U is for Uncle Sam.
   Don't forget to mention
he is not a real man
   but an old cartoon invention.

Uncle Sam is a political cartoon character that has personified the United States since the 1800s, when Thomas Nast and other political cartoonists began to draw him. Uncle Sam is more than a patriotic figure made famous in wartime recruiting posters. He is an important emblem in the dialogue between citizenry and government. Uncle Sam is a symbol of the right to free speech, for those who wish to criticize government policies as well as those who want to express support.

When many citizens were protesting strongly against the Vietnam War in the 1960s, a new amendment emerged from the tumult and unrest. The Twenty-Sixth Amendment lowered the voting age from 21 to 18, which was the same age at which people could be drafted into the army.

Think about the word "patriot." It is interesting to contemplate the idea that the citizens who use their First Amendment rights to exercise an open dialogue with our government by expressing their views against a war, are being patriotic.

Uu

V is for the Voters.
When people use their voices,
they get the best results
by expressing their own choices.

PLACE VOTE HERE

Citizenry is like the fourth branch of government because of the important dialogue we the people have through our elected officials. Voting is a crucial part of this process.

More than 2,500 years ago the ancient Greeks were among the first people to vote. They usually voted by raising their hands, but later, the Romans started using secret ballots. Privacy in voting is a right we still safeguard today.

American-born and naturalized citizens can vote in this country, but you must fill out a voter registration form first. It includes things like your name and address, and even though some states ask about which political party you belong to, you don't have to say. You can register as an independent. All voters are free to check off candidates from any party on the ballot. You must be 18 years of age or older to vote in a local, state, or national election.

Imagine yourself at the Constitutional Convention in 1787. You have been selected as a delegate to help come up with a plan for our new government. Hugh Williamson is there from North Carolina. He suggests that we have a king. Thomas Jefferson vehemently disagrees, preferring an elected president. This subject alone was voted on 60 times. George Washington ran unopposed as our first president.

This gives you an idea of how our democratic system of government, where the Constitution guarantees every citizen's civil liberties, did not happen spontaneously. The Founding Fathers worked long and hard to hammer out a design for our government.

The president is the head of our democracy, in charge of the executive branch of the federal government. To be elected president you must be at least 35 years old, an American-born citizen, and have lived in the United States for the last 14 years. The elected term is four years long. The president's yearly salary started at $25,000 and has been raised periodically over the years. Today it is $400,000. Once a year the president must give a speech called the State of the Union, which lets everyone know how the country is doing.

W is for George Washington
and presidents down the years.
For working long and working hard,
we give them all three cheers!

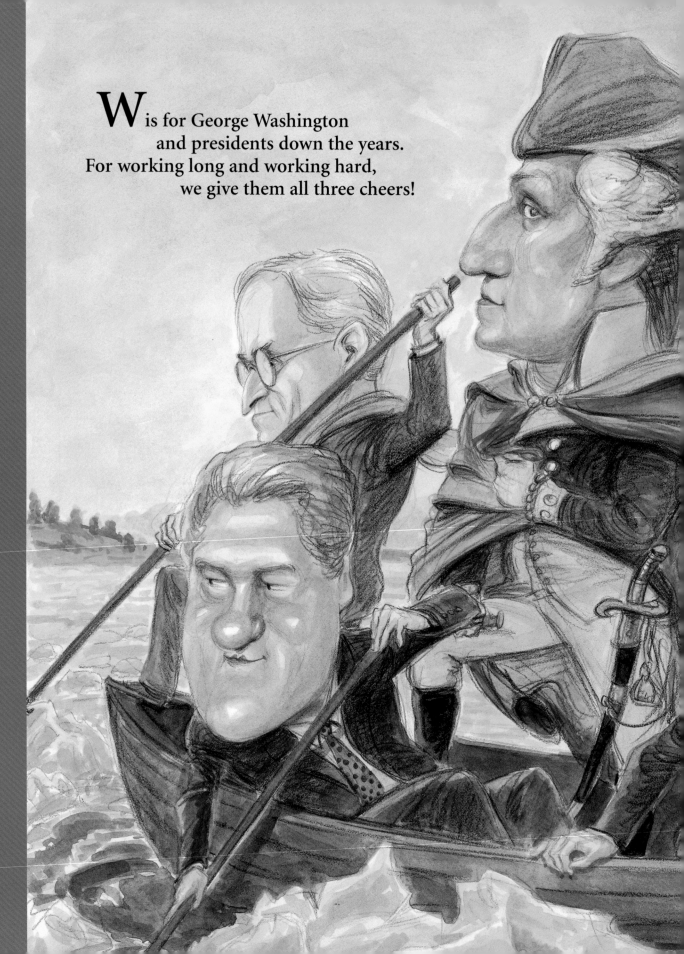

The executive branch of the federal government includes 15 departments, among them the Departments of Education, Agriculture, Defense, and Health. The president chooses whom he wants to be in charge of each department, but the Senate has to approve them (checks and balances!).

If you want to contact the president, you can write to the White House, 1600 Pennsylvania Avenue, Washington, D.C. 20502.

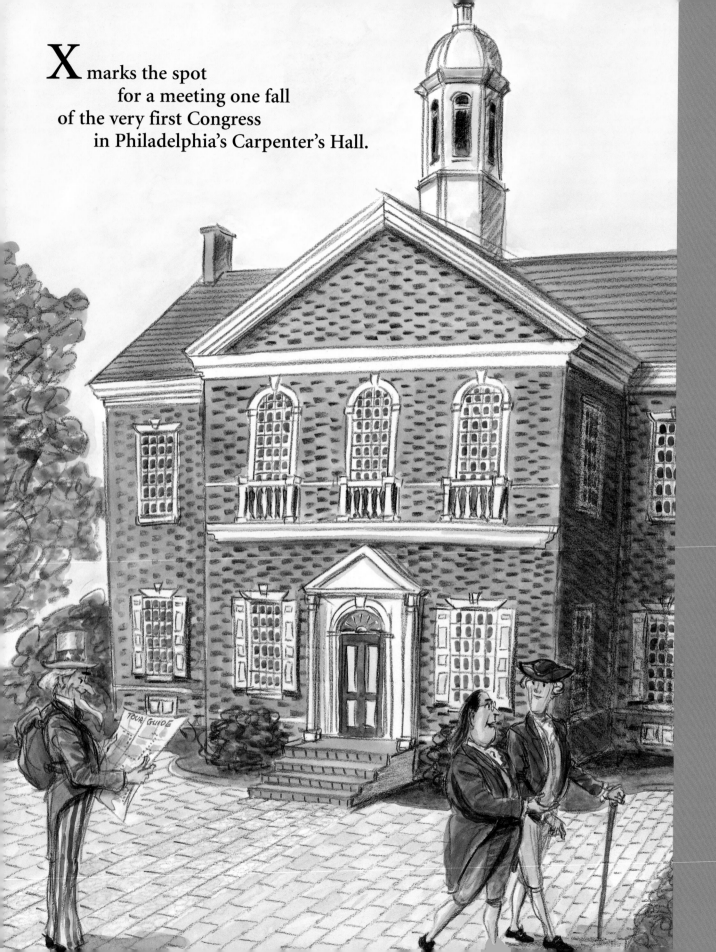

X marks the spot
for a meeting one fall
of the very first Congress
in Philadelphia's Carpenter's Hall.

When the early colonists came to America in search of more economic and religious freedom, they had a bumpy road ahead. The King of England was reluctant to grant them free trade. He didn't want to lose all that business! When the king tried to corner the market on tea, the colonists protested by dumping three English cargo ships full of tea into the Boston Harbor. This was known as the Boston Tea Party.

The First Continental Congress was held at Carpenter's Hall in Philadelphia in 1774. It was a meeting among 56 delegates from the 13 colonies (Georgia chose not to participate) to find a way to still stay under English rule but create a situation of economic independence. They wanted to find a compromise position with the king. Only a handful of radicals proposed breaking away from England at that time. The result of the meeting was to create an association to boycott (refuse to buy) English products.

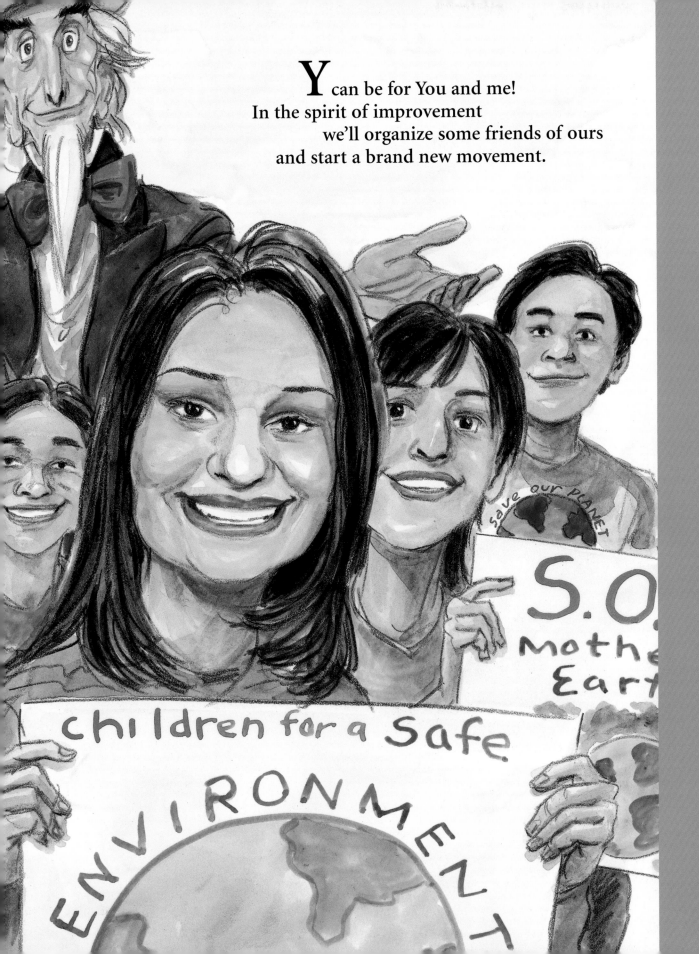

Y can be for You and me!
In the spirit of improvement
we'll organize some friends of ours
and start a brand new movement.

Yy

In 1988 Kory Johnson, a nine-year-old girl from Arizona, started a group called Children for a Safe Environment. Kory's sister Amy had died a few months earlier, after a lifetime of being sick. Their mother had unknowingly drunk well water contaminated by industrial cleaners during her pregnancy with Amy, and that was the cause of her death.

Kory has been organizing people to keep polluters out of poor neighborhoods ever since. She speaks all over the country. In 1998 when Kory was 19, she won a major environmental award for her important work. Children for a Safe Environment is an example of a 'grassroots' movement. This is when an individual or group of ordinary citizens initiates a change in the way things work, sometimes even a change in the law.

Indeed, the United States is regarded all over the world for its grassroots spirit. Are there examples of grassroots movements in your community?

Z is for the Zeitgeist,
the excitement in the air.
There was hard work ahead
with freedom to declare.

WE WANT YOU TO GET

INVOLVED

Zeitgeist is a German word, translating as "time spirit," meaning the feeling or spirit of a certain period of time. (It rhymes with "night heist.") When we talk about the Zeitgeist of the early days of America, think about the remarkable people of the time and the dramatic adventure on which they were embarking. History does not often see such a brilliant, forward-thinking group of minds. You have read about some of the Founding Fathers who worked long and hard to forge American democracy. The "spirit of the time" was embodied by women, as well.

Abigail Adams (1744-1818) was the wife of our second president, John Adams, and the mother of our sixth president, John Quincy Adams. Mrs. Adams was one of the most influential First Ladies. She was a loud advocate for education for women and fiercely opposed slavery. Deborah Sampson (1760-1827) disguised herself as a man so she could join the Massachusetts army, where she fought bravely alongside other soldiers in the Revolutionary War. Mary Hays McCauly (1754-1832) and Margaret Corbin (1751-1800) distinguished themselves by their remarkable bravery during that war, as well, when they joined their husbands on the battlefield, and helped win our country's fight for independence.

Who or what will shape the Zeitgeist of your generation?

Zz

You, Too, Are A Citizen!
Getting Involved With Democracy

*You may not yet be old enough to cast your vote in a political election but there are still ways in which you can participate in our democratic society. Read the following tips and projects and decide how **you** can be an active citizen.*

Feed Your Brain

Become informed about some of the things going on around you. Know what's happening!

★ Read a newspaper or a current events magazine, especially the local editorial/opinion page. What are the issues other citizens are concerned with? Follow the issues and what others are writing about it. Are any related to your area? Mark "hot spots" on a map.

★ Watch the news with a friend or a family member and then talk about what you have seen.

★ Listen to what others are talking about when meeting with friends and family at school or church or other social activities.

Stay informed. Follow an issue that matters to you—the building or paving-over of a park, leash laws for dogs, laws regulating skateboarding, etc...

★ Know both sides of the issue.

★ Where is the issue being discussed—editorial page, city council meetings, planning commission meetings? Join the dialogue either actively or as a citizen who wants to be better informed.

★ Discuss the issue with the people who might be making the decisions such as your school principal or counselor, local clergy, or city council person.

Understand your rights and respect the rights of others.

★ Ask family members if they know the three R's of being a good citizen: the Right to have and express your own opinion, Respect for other peoples' rights, and the Responsibility to protect the rights of every citizen.

★ Read the Bill of Rights.

Use Your Voice

Ask questions at the dinner table about current events. Form ideas of your own. Start a dialogue with your parents to understand how they feel about events.

Play a game in your classroom. Pretend you are news reporters and have everyone take turns thinking of a subject they would like to report on: water pollution in your town's rivers and lakes? Skateboard laws? Better laws against noise pollution? What would you like to change?

Write an editorial/opinion letter to your local newspaper that helps focus peoples' attention on something you think should be changed or improved.

★ Send a copy of your letter to your schoolteacher so it can be part of classroom discussion.

★ Ask others who share your views to also write letters.

★ Write a letter to your local selectmen, mayor, or city council representative about something you think should be changed in your community. A need for nighttime lighting in your neighborhood park? Money to fix up the local playground? Your letter will get read, and you might even get a reply.

If you like to do art projects, make a poster or sign for a particular cause and let it do the talking for you.

Take Some Action

Join your school's student council board. Become knowledgeable about what is of interest and importance to your fellow students. What do *you* think is important to your school?

Along with your parents, attend a city council meeting or school board meeting. What decisions are being made that affect you? How can you help influence your community into making the right decisions?

Attend a local voting center: When elections take place in your local community, ask your parents if you can accompany them when they go to cast their vote. This "family night out" serves two purposes: First, it reminds your parents to vote. Second, when you attend and see the voting process firsthand, you get an idea of how the system works and its importance in our society.

Volunteer to make a change for the better. Organize a food drive. Collect food in your school or community for nearby homeless shelters. How many old books do you have that you don't read anymore? Organize a book-drive for children in shelters and others who can't afford to buy them. Start a recycling awareness program and collect cans and donate the money raised. Don't forget to tell the local newspaper about your event.

Learn more about the local and regional organizations in your area and what they are doing to make better/stronger/healthier communities. What can you do to help their efforts? Let the decision-makers know your opinion. In our democracy our leaders rely upon citizens voicing their opinions. Let your local leaders know your opinion and *why* you have that opinion. You *can* make a difference!

Examples of Making a Change

Annie Wignall started her own organization at age 11, called Care Bags Foundation. It provided some basic items like toothbrushes and age-appropriate games and books, to disadvantaged, homeless, or abused kids. Local agencies distributed the bags to 80 towns, all over her state of Iowa.

Joshua Marcus was the CEO of his own company at age 14. He started Sack it to You! which raised $250,000 to purchase school supplies and backpacks for needy students in Boca Raton, Florida.

Eleven-year-old Stacey Hillman read an article in the newspaper about the dangers police dogs face, and how there were bullet-proof vests available for the dogs but the police department could not afford them. She started Pennies to Protect Dogs. In two years Stacey's organization raised over $100,000—which was enough for bulletproof vests for 158 K-9 dogs.

Zachary Ebers came up with the idea for Breakfast Bonanza at age 14. His organization collected over 5,000 boxes of cereal for food pantries all over St. Louis, Missouri.

Twelve-year-old Charlie Shufeldt, of Atlanta, Georgia, and his friends Owen Boger and Josh Silfen, founded Free Bytes, an organization that collects used computer equipment. They donate the equipment to non-profit organizations who can't afford to buy it new, and then high school students volunteer to restore the equipment for its new owners.

Elissa Grodin

Elissa Grodin attended Dartmouth College and the School of Visual Arts. She has written for the *Times Literary Supplement* and *New Statesman*. She met her husband, Charles Grodin, when she interviewed him for *American Film* magazine.

In talking about her work on *D is for Democracy: A Citizen's Alphabet*, Elissa says, "Working on *D is for Democracy* was immensely satisfying. The research and writing afforded me the dual pleasure of teaching myself as well as my readers about our system of government and its bewitching history, crammed with men and women of brilliance and originality. It was unavoidably inspiring."

D is for Democracy is her second children's book with Sleeping Bear Press. She also wrote *N is for Nutmeg: A Connecticut Alphabet*. Elissa lives with her family in Wilton, Connecticut.

Victor Juhasz

A graduate of the Parsons School of Design, Victor Juhasz began illustrating in 1974 while still a student and has been working nonstop ever since. His humorous illustrations and caricatures have been commissioned by major magazines, newspapers, advertising agencies, and book publishers, both national and international, and his clients include *Time*, *Newsweek*, the *New Yorker*, *Rolling Stone*, the *New York Times*, the *Washington Post*, *GQ*, and Warner Books.

Victor lives and works in Elizabeth, New Jersey, with his wife, Terri, a psychotherapist. He has three grown sons, Max, Alex, and Ben. *D is for Democracy* is his first children's book in over 20 years.